COOKING THE
STARS

A COLLECTION OF POEMS BY SAM BAILEY

authorHOUSE®

AuthorHouse™
1663 Liberty Drive
Bloomington, IN 47403
www.authorhouse.com
Phone: 1-800-839-8640

Published by AuthorHouse 2/12/2013

ISBN: 978-1-4817-1384-9 (sc)
ISBN: 978-1-4817-1385-6 (e)

Library of Congress Control Number: 2013902672

CONSIDER THIS

poets in their imaginary kitchens
with their imaginary pots
cooking the stars
bubbling the heavens
watching the constellations rise
universal cooks
creating brand new dishes
perfecting the ingredients

TABLE OF CONTENTS

FIELDS GONE BY

we might not have cared so much
had we not somehow known
those smokey fields where battles played
so quickly overgrown
with dry thin grass and thorny shade
that only shadows touch

and we might not have known so much
had we not felt or heard
the clash of angry men and seen
a bloody mockingbird
limping through those fields obscene
where only shadows touch

if only those who perished there
upon that dry thin grass
had known the awful price absurd
that they would pay to pass
the shadow of that mockingbird
ahead for us to share

now shadows shadows everywhere
our souls are overwhelmed
by hollow wind and thorns and grass
and memories filled at last
with ancient bones and empty skies
and all those fields gone by

LIFELINE

our ship rides on light
under a kaleidoscopic sky
sails spill reflections that sparkle
in storms of fractured colors and shapes

throw out the line
let it grab and pull
and anchor us here
midst the swells and the spray

and anchor us here
where the light is true
'till the days and the storms
and our lives are through

PARADE OF THE BOATS

she died quietly
a few days ago
end of a meaningful life
with many friends and a large family
the loved wife of a lobsterman
who had his own parade years ago
now it's her time
as seventeen boats large and small
move slowly down the river
in a random arrangement of honor
quietly past christmas cove
pemaquid beach and point
and finally at sea
they stop to form a wheel
with bows pointing out and sterns in
a joined circle of boats
her ashes are carefully placed
upon the water in the center
flowers are cast
and then the hush is broken
by seventeen horns in tribute
shattering the sky

STORM AT SEA

The stiffening breeze
moves jetsam
discarded through years
of careless change.

Then frantic winds
whirl and lose direction
as the cargo
of life's remembrances

rocks and shifts,
seeking stability...
longing for quiet.

Finally,
the dying wind
allows all things
to settle,

and the sea rests...
a slow
sweet
calm.

RECOVERY

Shapes changed that day
when worry found a way
to cross our shores.
Wounds opened
and the steam of rushing blood
dimmed our sight,
stained our minds,
condensed on the cold
bare framework
of our souls.

Now, years have gone,
the lost are found
or the found are lost...
(one cannot say.)
But the blood, though set,
still lies
behind our eyes,
obscuring
and confusing
the way.

MEDALS FOR THE BRAVE

if we had offered
they would have shrugged
turned their backs
and walked away

undoing the result of evil
earns no award
(they would have said)
not until its very root
was pulled and shredded
would they present
with smiles
and shoulders squared

but now
because they can't refuse
give them at least
medals of horror

just lay one on each grave

ALONE

after so many years
family
meetings and work
holidays and vacations
the whole busy business
all gone now
even an old love
who is miles away
and mostly unattainable
cannot assuage the emptiness
of an uninhabited life
sadness nearly overwhelms
as days begin to fade
and memories start to echo
off the imagined walls
of some cold and barren room

HITCH HIKER

it started in a deep pool
eons ago
now your steps
lead you to a canteen
lost beside the road
and the driver
coming back to find it
stops and offers you a ride
all diagramed
as just another step
or line in a pattern
that must develop
so dream
but drift within your scope
accept what is
and enjoy

DEMENTIA

it crawled on her ceiling
made a sound in her hand
and the tangles and plaques
formed a convoluted web
a coagulation of misplaced sensibilities

the spider moved quietly
at the center
feeling for things lost
feeding on pieces of self
finally leaving only her smile
nothing more

DRUNKEN RIVER

falling down the hillside
staggering between winding banks
under boughs of disapproving trees
tripping on rocks
then slowing
and sliding
through rainbowed mist
into trembling eddies and pools
nervously awaiting
the next confused decent

APOLOGIES TO SHAKESPEARE

Let me not to the carriage of two blinds
Admit impediments; use no gloves
Which alter when they alteration find,
Or bend with the remover to remove.
The blinds, if properly fixed and sharp
Will look on tempests and be not shaken
And shelter all from every howl and bark
Which might cause fright and major quakin'.
A glove's a fine tool though rusty pips and creaks
Within its rending, tearing efforts come;
A glove alters not with its brief hours and weeks
But shields the wearer even to the edge of doom.

    If this be error and upon me proved,
    I never writ, nor no man ever gloved.

APOLOGIES TO MILTON

When I consider how my leg is bent
ere half way down this dark stair and wide,
and that one limb which is death to slide
lodged with me useless to become more bent
and thus can serve no more my body or present
a true account, I to the other leg must chide:
"They can't expect full-labor, one leg denied,"
I fondly state. But Patience, to prevent
that murmur, soon replies, "You do not need
both legs. What bears you best
will serve you best. Your state
is singly. A millipede at speed
can post o'er land and ocean without rest,
but you can serve 'tho standing wobbly and not straight."

DINING IN

in a quiet corner of the kitchen
the distorted greasy light
spills sloppily on the table
touching work worn hands
that rest carelessly now
midst the momentaneous mess
of a butchered meal
not enjoyed or savored
but simply used by bodies
too tired to care
elemental stuff
shoved
not spooned
or forked
or even cut
but fingered in
and then forgotten

LAMENT OF A BAPTIST AT A FUNDAMENTALIST CLAMBAKE

god is hungry
ain't it rich
he's just another version
of a son of a bitch
who makes a shambles
of things gone wrong
like pain and illness
anger and shame
and gives them
a half life of eons and more
then hunts us forever
with dark open jaws
until we're digested
in an infinite black maw

IT MAY BE TOO LATE...

the Devil's in charge
and there's nothing but hate,
our hearts are numb,
and our souls are on fire.
When the world's like this
the whole damned land
is ready to kiss
the Devil's hot hand.
Do you think our tears
might subtly plumb
the depths of evil
and restore the green
or embellish the dark
with humanity's sheen?
Do you think if we tried,
we might drown him in tears?
Do you think if we cried
it would help and the years
of hatred and fear
would just disappear?
If the Devil's in charge
and there's nothing but hate,
in spite of our tears
it may be too late.

THE DEVIL AT EASTER

be gone horned creature
you're not wanted here
you're nothing but trouble
nothing but fear and
pain for the masses
(hope for a few)

I've got no room
for trivia like you
the month of april
is pregnant again
with rebirth
goodwill
the triad
and sin

so it worries me not
the state that you're in
for my soul is well-worn
with a resonant skin
and can never be torn
by some devilish whim

HAWK

soft strong circles
in a quiet sky
we look up knowing
the hawk's yellow eyes
saw us long ago

she says
it would be cool
to be a hawk
but I wonder
how cool

to always be
watching
searching
waiting
and then

to eat mice

HELIOS

it was a slow burning
of the land
of life
for we had no hoses long enough
to control the invisible fire

the earth
was cracked
and dry
even the air
too arid to breathe

the sun
demanded
genuflection
as it took more and more control
of all that remained alive

the rains came
with life and promise
but we bowed in fear
knowing above the clouds
the chariot still crossed the sky

NO QUESTIONS ASKED

a light April rain dampened the crunch
of my footsteps on the gravel driveway
shrubs on both sides
showed damage from the winter
but mostly from the deer
how can such a beautiful animal
be such a pest?
stopped by the local sports store
to get a slingshot
stood in the pistol and rifle section
between crossbows
and bows and arrows
and was told that slingshots
are banned in New Jersey
because they are considered to be
terrorist weapons
went online
had one sent from Colorado
no questions asked

IT WANES TOO SOON

that's the thing
about the moon

its fullness surprises
then wanes too soon

it should set slowly
with its orange glow

like a fall camp fire
in the woods below

turning dark at the edge
where it touches the earth

I've seen it full
many times before

and felt it pull
the tides onshore

and the tides that slide
and roll inside

but it sets so fast
I always run

to find someone
to share with me

this fleeting glimpse
of mortality

GOLDFINCH

tiny yellow flyer
flickering like a flame
pursued by golden friends and foes
in a crazy headlong rush
you dive through leaves and branches
without a nick or scrape
and move so fast one would expect
your flame would catch and spread
and if you somehow land to rest
it's not for long because
the others whirl around you
and the rush is on again

my thoughts at least can join you
and quickly learn to fly
in my imagination
we'll blaze brightly you and I
and in a blur of color
race madly through the sky

PORTLAND CEMENT

the incipient vitrification
of a calcareous
or
argillaceous soul
caused
by
disuse
or
the cold
of reality
troubles only a few
because
like many diseases
it is hard to
recognize
but
we might
finely
grind the clinker
and
make something
universally useful

SEEDLING

Planted years ago
at the edge
of the lawn
our wedding favor
a seedling
now a sturdy pine
still growing
nearly grown
will they sell
its lumber
when it's done?
will they keep
our lumber
when we're gone?

SEASONS

the winter white
goes down
wherever water might

beside a road
within a stream
it all goes down

until one day
a rusty pump
or pulley

brings it up
to wet the dry
and dusty lips of summer

then summer shakes off sweat
that falls upon the ground
and it all goes down

round and round
the seasons change
the circle wins

it always will
and we
we all go down

DON'T FEEL SORRY FOR THE CAT

we will never know the cause
for she'll not condescend or pause
to let us know her deepest thoughts
instead she'll simply walk with care
one paw held slightly in the air
her halting strange tripodal gait
still seeming dignified and straight
what used to be her fearful prey
now watch her move and seem to say
a huntress without four good feet
is doomed to realize defeat
but how could they so soon forget
that what still lies behind her grin
is a mouth chock full of glistening teeth
and also waiting there beneath
something else to give them pause
a full three feet of lethal claws

A BETTER PLACE

Such a shame,
to never see again
a sky like this, so blue,
so clean and clear,
a backdrop for the early leaves
and piercing white
of the dogwood trees...
to never see young flowers
shift silently
in the languid breeze,
and the sun so warm,
the sun so warm.

All this you'll never see again,
so I guess I'll have to see for you
as I thank each day
for what it is
and for what you were.
And when they say
there's a better place,
I'll have to wonder
how that can be...
what better place
is there, my love,
than the place
right here with me?

THE LAST WHITE BEAR

though still young
he leans
and then slowly falls
and the august-like earth
puffs and rises
around the last white bear

his great tears run
through the light coat of dust
until a warm february-arrow
pierces his soul
and freezes his heart

lowering the bow
we ask in horror
how could it happen?

SMALL TOWN

On a quiet street with a quiet beat
growing up was a sheltered blur,
for as far as we knew
bad things that occurred
were elsewhere things, and few,
except for the little bumps and zings
neither we nor our parents could hide.

When somebody put
a gun in his mouth,
we heard it, then asked our folks,
and were told in response,
a truck had backfired...
all's well, it's ok.
And the scariest thing:
the paper next day
had nothing at all to say.

But what happened that day
tore a hole in the dark
and suddenly made us aware.
Suppose he had talked
and been listened to,
suppose somebody had cared.
Was his life a blur,
was it sheltered and still,
was it wisdom that nobody heard?

Hiding the truth
was a hazardous thing,
and learning was all up to us,
so, in spite of our fears,
we listened to him,
and grew wiser and wiser each year.

POOR PLUTO, POOR ME

What's the answer
when there is none,
when a star's indiscretion
causes a dog named
piece of rock
to be cast out
and declared
mini?

We learned
there were nine...
What do I do now,
revise my entire
youth? Pretend
it never happened?
Easy for
some scientist to do...

But not for me.
All this time
I've been waiting
for number ten
and it's damned difficult
to suddenly find
I'm really waiting
for number nine.

SURPRISING CALM

here I lie
with a kind of detached reverence
watching the line
snake carefully
into my heart…
a half hour later
I'll be joking with the nurses
and two days after that
buying plumbing supplies
but right now
be carcful if you will
we're talking millimeters

had it been the left side
not the right
or had I remembered
to take my watch off
before I hit the floor…
those slight changes
might have done me in entirely
but since deviations years ago
probably fashioned
today's inevitability
acceptance comes without fear
and with surprising calm

PARMETER'S BARN

It rests on a hill,
just an outline now,
with huge shadowed openings
where time has removed
blood red chunks
of the ancient wood.
We expected it tall
and all in one piece,
instead it looks torn
and chewed by some beast.

Back then, you could see it
from miles away...
coming back from a trip
we'd always say:
there's Parmeter's barn,
we're home at last.

Now, we look through the walls
at what's left inside...
rusty tools, empty stalls,
some hay, a scythe...
and our dusty memories slide and sway
on the hazy hint of an earlier day
when the fields were full
and the sun was high
and the barn was young
and could blot out the sky.

DOUBT

Going home
the perfect way
would be straight,
as fast as possible,
not looking to the sides,
just plain straight.
Or would a few bends
and sideways glances
be better?
Would we rather know
or be oblivious to it all?
If we knew,
we might have to stop
and lend a hand.
We'll know the answer
when we're home.

ESCALATOR

Approaching with care,
looking down the stair,
near two lovely
young girls who are
standing there,
I smile and then
happily wave
them on first,
get smiles in return
and nods of thanks.
Do they think
I'm chivalrous,
trying to be
nice? Hell no,
it's done just
to make perfectly sure
that if I lose my balance
and start to fall,
I'll have
something to stop me,
something soft,
that's all.

HOTEL

Hotel in Boston,
twentieth floor,
sound asleep at 3AM...
stentorian alarm
urgently tells us
without delay
to use the stairs
to the street.
An hour later
cleared to return,
on elevators now,
to our rooms.

Down to breakfast
with the couple
next door,
all of us proper
and carefully dressed,
our shins aching
from the downward climb,
but laughing
about meeting
hours before
dressed in night clothes
and not much more.

Then a shadow flickers
in the backs of our minds,

it might have been real,
it could have been real...
but a shrug is enough
to remind us all
they wouldn't build anything half as tall
if they thought for a moment
it ever might fall...

NEVER LIE TO THE TOOTH FAIRY

When Sam lost a tooth
and it fell to the floor
the dog got it first
and then ran out the door.
At about the same time,
Sam's mom standing near
felt the pull of the moon
and something quite queer:
her molar broke suddenly,
cusps and all,
but she managed to catch it
before it could fall.

Sam looked at her quizzically
and she looked at him,
and they wondered together,
would the tooth fairy know?
Switching big tooth for little,
would the difference show?
Better write a note,
Sam's mother said,
never lie to the tooth fairy
when you're going to bed....
It's much, much smarter
to make arrangements instead.

So Sam got a pencil
and carefully wrote:
Ms Fairy, dear fairy,
I hope you don't mind
but the tooth that I lost
I just cannot find.
So in place of that one
here is another,
a great big thing
that belonged to my mother.
When it comes to its worth
if you feel there's not any,
perhaps from your heart
you'd just leave a penny.

That night when the tooth fairy
stopped by to look,
she checked under Sam's pillow
and immediately shook
when she saw the huge tooth
and the room that it took.
My goodness, she cried,
the child might have lied
and expected a ransom
for something this size!
But I've read the note
and it's safe to surmise
little Sam, after all,
deserves a big prize.

Thus ends the story
of Sam's missing tooth...
the moral, quite simply,
is just tell the truth.

If you try to deceive
you'd best be wary,
for you'll never ever fool
the old tooth fairy.

INFECTION

invaders, prepare...
Lord Levaquin rides hard within my vessels
to seek out your surly nest
there to smite thee one by one
and thus erase thy presence
and its effect upon the climate
and wellbeing of my assaulted state
you hit me hard but now it's yours to falter
as my protector scatters your spiteful hoard
and returns the thermostat from 103
to a far far kinder 99

HAVE YOUR CHILD DO IT FOR YOU

When did it happen,
the young ones
born with full-blown
computer savvy?
You call a business
and are told to go
online
to get your answer,
or,
if you don't know how,
have your child do it for you.
Now we get insults
from machines!
Are they programming
themselves,
or is it still
humans
with a vicious
sense of humor
who have flipped it all
upside down,
the base on top
the top below
teetering on a point
in the softness
of this crazy world?

Perhaps
we
need
to
reboot…

IF AFTER ALL

if after all you go before
and we do not take
those first careful steps together
going down
into the vast dark valley
that rolls and rolls
to the distant hills so far away
and if only later I am drawn
one way or another
to where you are
where neither of us
will ever leave
then oh then
however long I've had to wait
the sadness will have been
so deep
and the space between
so wide
I pray somehow
that even though you go before
and even though I stay alone
eternity
will be time enough
eternity will be time enough

PLAYTIME

Soldiers, marching near the edge,
Arranged in perfect ranks,
With lines and movements ordered by
A youngish general who
Has organized his army from
The image in his head
Derived from moving pictures
And the war books he has read.
Unfeeling, metal soldiers
Marching always at the whim
Of an eight year old commander who
Forgets the state he's in.
By platoon, company, battalion,
He orders them to fall
From the table where they're gathered
To the floor, yes, one and all.
Retrieved, they muster once again
And wait for his command,
Then silently they march until
They're on the floor again.
What scares me more than I can say
Is knowing what may be
In forty years or so when he's
Not playing fast and free,
We just might see his troops once more
March boldly to the fore,
And silently, at his command,
All end up on the floor.

SECOND CHANCE

It's not what he is,
It's not what they are…
It's a moon shifting shadows
Under some distant star,
Near a world, slowly idling,
That slips into gear
And moves with a beat
Only some of us hear.
The land of the living
Is far…Oh so far…
And that moon bathed in starlight
Reflects on a world
Where something exceptional,
Trying to be born,
Weaves the moonlight
Into patterns and forms,
Creating a scaffold, a matrix for life,
Not as we are
And not as we were,
But as we should be
Under some fresh, young star.

HOUSE

the house stands and hides
the man who makes his way inside
he built it with lies
and misconceptions
pulled tight the windows
locked the doors
and felt secure in darkness
but if he thinks about his world
and wonders what it's all about
he'll need the light
he'll cry and claw the air
fist out windows
kick out doors
and we the wise ones
should we come to help
will find the house has snapped its frame
and crushed the man inside

BROKEN ROAD

spread my bones
on that broken road
spread my bones
and fill the cracks
spread my bones
so the road's not broke
and my soul is whole
and the world is right
then take what's left
just grab what's there
and cast those bones
on the breeze somewhere

ICE

the afternoon sun of winter
is a spot of off-red coolness
that shines on the surface of clear ice
with sheens of crystal stillness

the skater glides in the silence
his shadow
a featureless thing
making no sound in its motion

as it slides with a careful ease
over something
a darkness
a feeling

and the off-red sun of winter
worries men to the ice
where skaters glide on that feeling
unaware
    unafraid
        half dead

MUD

If you lie on your back
In the ooze, deliciously,
Playfully happy,
With rain softly splashing
On your face,
and little things under
and around you
In the mud…
A surge of sudden
Selflessness and sureness
May course down your flanks
And around your legs,
And slowly, caressingly,
Enter the vessels of your feet
To burst forth
In ten tiny tinkles
Through your toes
Upthrust from the mud
In a kind of idiotic denial.
If you do that, with the breeze
Tickling your soles,
You, with a grin,
Quite probably will forget
How deep and dark the mud is.

SHADOWS IN GLASS

I walked that street one night
and that night it was lonely and bare
as the hollow wet wind moved the light
over lines and cracks in the walk
and the cast of the dim light
the cast of the maunder light
made puddles seem so deep

years later as I walk that street
comes a childhood sound
of lightly crinkling glass wind chimes
whose sharp broken harmony
prickles my soul and fills the empty street
with shapes and forms
that only my crystal thought can see

A ROSE BY ANY OTHER NAME

a rose of another color
might be the same
but would it smell as sweet
if it had another name?

If it were named vomit
or carcinogen
wouldst thou even then
bring thy nose to sniff?

I thinkest not
for other flowers 'neath the sky
would rightly warrant then
profound exposure to thine eye

and the ill-named vomit bush
carcinogenic to us all
would stand alone boughed in shame
as summer turned to fall

ANOTHER PARTY

People sit around and make words,
And laugh and say,
"Do you want something more?"
Or read poetry and think
They are knowing each other,
While really all they want to know is,
"What does your father do?"

HILL

walking the hill
in younger years
a simple easy climb
but now the reach
to lustrous air
seems higher than before
and all things said
or done through time
lie like crumbs
making a path
that we in failing light
must follow best we can
but walking that hill
is a struggle now
and the birds will come
and find the crumbs

MIRROR

The yellowed edge of time
Spreads out to touch
Our newest age.
Things that were past
Now reach again to find
Their new beginning...
Now reach for us,
The young, bright boys,
Who, hypnotized, step
Lightly backward, trying
To retain our boyish freedom.

Yet, somehow we know
That edge will lap
And clutch our dancing feet,
Not stilling them...
But guiding into wars,
Through peace, through life,
To death. Tomorrow's but a mirror...
Reverse the image
And agree with me
That yesterday is to begin...
Today is gone...

It's all the same.

THE GAME

You are not free.
You cannot spin
Your world at will.
A hand grips your world
And holds it hard.
It holds the way
Buildings of steel are held…
Insensibly rigid,
Ideas enmeshed in form.
Your world is held
With knuckled grip
And you gulp air in disbelief
And fiercely try
To spin the top
That skids away.
A child spins tops with ease…
You've lost the knack
And fight with tears
To tear away some hand
That stops your world,
But all in vain.
You fool!
The hand you hold that holds you,
Is your own.

WEATHER REPORT

Seriously cloudy
(sez the man)
Partial clearing
(sez the man)
Rain
(sez the man)
Snow
(sez the man)
Fog
(sez the man)

So what
(sez I)

I get paid
(sez the man)

So continue
(sez I)

TRANSITION
(A FATHER SPEAKS TO
HIS CHILDREN)

my long sweet song
is almost done
dampened now like piano strings
when that strange third pedal
is pressed
notes fall away
hollowed from too much use
and too many years
some sadness
as the tune ends
but comfort to know
it's your time now
and in years ahead
you and yours
will climb the hills
sing your songs
and play your notes
all crystal and new
I only pray
the world will hear in yours
faint echoes at least
of mine

THREE CINQUAINS

A lamp,
A radio,
And a chair. Radio
Playing…lamp on…but her chair is
Empty.

My face
Bobs back and forth,
Keeps time with lively notes,
Then darkens when the music ends.
She's gone.

Ashes…
A fireplace,
Last night the logs glowed and
Warmed our love. Now the ashes are
My tears.

COMMENT ONE

When at last a day is done,
should a man forget?
Should he pat the fur
and kiss the lips
and settle for a pipe
and chair and fire?
Or should he hate the day,
and remember how he felt
in the elevator,
or as he stood
before some smartass
with a painted face
smiling: in just one minute…
Then, at least,
he was alive,
if only in anger.
That was something.

BACK TO SCHOOL

Am going back to school this year
For going get some praise
Is going not to school just nights
Instead go full-time days

Some others think is crazy nut
I might agree some but
Is going back to school real soon
In fact think maybe June

How often has you thought of such
To better self through school
For sitting here ain't learning much
If not go back is fool

But going back to school you say
Ain't right the way you are
Well you keep sit on seat of pants
You sure not going far

Chew iron nails make shatter teeth
Scream Foul and blubber tears
Just don't sit tight with placid smile
You do you murder years

For all we got is what can be
What's now count not one bit
You narrow look you miss a lot
And worse you narrow be

So join me back to school this year
Join me in search for us
Look wide at all there is with me
We will be what can be

RATS ON GOOD AND EVIL

Beauty the cat was all heart,
And somehow her kindness
Rubbed off on the dog.
When Snoopy, the rat,
Disowned her puppies,
Beauty, big heart,
Suckled all five.

Recently Beauty ate a blue lizard,
And, paralyzed, the good heart died.
What of Beauty's litter of kittens?
Snoopy the dog looked on for a while,
Then she took over their care and feeding.

Snoopy the dog,
The rat, the louse,
Did what was done...
Not out of sympathy,
Not as a payment.
She, too, was all heart,
Yes, hers was a big heart,
Even Snoopy, the dog.

APOLOGIES TO THOMAS WOLFE

of course you can go home again
of course you can go home
though time has changed each town and field
has changed all that you knew
the basic thread of what you were
is whole and well and true

of course you can go home again
of course you can go home
though things appear quite different now
your ghosts remember you
and how you were in other days
when everything was new

of course you can go home again
of course you can go home
when you recall those memories
your thoughts will quickly roam
through all the magic of that time
and suddenly you'll be home

JAZZ

Jazz, man, jazz.
That's us, man, jazz.
Laughing and shouting
And kneeing and spouting
Words in dithyrambs,
In unholy screeblambs.

My head is a bongo,
Your hair is a harp...
Like a D sprongo
Bam in E flarp.

THE EMPTY ROOM

The cluttered table
Stands inside
The empty room,
And the sun
Makes stairways
In the dust.

What man or woman
Last sat smiling
At that table,
Last sat gorged
And peaceful
In the empty room?

War has snuffed
The flaming
Vibrant life
That once
Moved brightly
Through the room.

It has
Minuted us
To bits and pieces
That now must climb
Stairways
In the dust.

OFFSPRING

Lie carefully in the womb
Little one. She'll still love you
Once she sees what you become,
But now, with no army at your side
She might quit-claim you...
Throw you in the River Inn.

Could she, bearing incipient evil,
If she knew, maintain
A loving smile? Or
Would she rush to find
The nearest coat hanger?

So lie carefully, little Adolf,
While she looks to name you.
And, since you cannot yet,
She'll pick out wallpaper
For your room and tiny boots
To strut in when you're born.

EPITAPH

The struggle kicked up clouds of dust,
And rumbled thunder shook the earth.
A man stood, one of many in the war,
And raised his blunderbuss to fire.

He shut his eyes and pulled,
And nothing happened.

Blind man and silent thunder box,
Lie now beneath hanged earth
In one low grave with one crude epitaph:
"Blunderbuss"

They shut their eyes in fear of doing...
And nothing happened.

AFTER A BATTLE

When we entered the town,
Walls stood on every side...
Walls and roads, but no people.
The roads were true and led somewhere,
The walls were high and strong...
Where were the people?

I lay with a cheek on the cool road
And saw, with one eye,
A small trickle of water
Sliding slowly across the road
To disappear beyond the edge
At the other side.

That's how it is with people,
I thought, they live
And then disappear
Beyond the edge of some road.
But I could feel
Their presence.

I rose, and a little boy,
Who had been hiding behind a wall,
Threw a stone and hit me,
And I yelled,
By God, there they are, and ready to die,
For I'm bigger than he is.

AN UNPOPULAR WAR

Man with a smile and a guitar
Hanging loose on your back,
Have you come to play a tune for us,
To fill our empty world with echos
Of some bright, mysterious way,
To make us see invisible things?

Ah, now we see reflections of the truth
In your black eyes...at first you fooled us,
But you are not other than you were,
As we had hoped. Our's is no beggar's role,
Our minds hold more than offered chaff...
We know you for a fraud.

Your discordant tune is only played
To hypnotize, to lead us to your late black world.
So, here's the deal:
Show us the truth in lies,
And we will follow you,
And thrive on death as you.

REGRETS

they fell on sandy beaches
iwo jima and omaha
incipient souls destroyed by chance
cut short from lives back home
unripened men whose ruined dreams
lay torn like blackened flags
but see them rise
these dead young ghosts
and move in endless rows
and watch their deadened marching
in the awful bloody sand
then hear them say
all would have changed
if only they had lived
they would have spun a special world
no sand
no pain
no death
it's sad for them they perished young
it's more than sad for us

COMMENT II

He wandered down the dirty street
Tripped and fell
Cutting his face
Far away from home
In a land foreign and unreal
He had paid his pack of smokes
For a release of sorts
Met the natives
And found them not too different
Two men from his unit found him
And took him back to his compound
Where wire fences
Enclosed a small bit of America

FOOTBALL NEAR THE DMZ

The sky was clear and the seats were free
the day we played football near the DMZ.
Across the line, behind the hills, anxiously waited the enemy,
anxiously waiting to see us play football near the DMZ.

The first half was done, so, needless to say,
the halftime show got underway.
Out came a soldier covered with pads
who started to jog, so we cheered the lad.

As we stood to watch the flight and the fun,
two handlers with dogs released them to run
after the jogger they considered a foe,
and the pads weren't enough, or he just ran too slow.

There's no reason for us to be sad that he died,
for the sky was still clear and the seats were still free,
and the enemy feared what they just couldn't see,
that day we played football near the DMZ.

CULTURE

A wonderful time of bright new days,
Of bugle sounds early, then exploring the ways
Of a culture quite backward and different from us,
Of people whose lives are not worth our trust.

We buried a tank in the field today...
The IG is coming, there'll be hell to pay
Since there's one tank too many and the quota's not right...
So we hid the damn thing right in plain sight.

In a country like this you never know
When you'll need one more tank even though
We don't need it to fight, we just need it for show.

If only their lives were worth our trust...
If only these people were as cultured as us.

SECURITY

Our compound's secure, we can't do any more.
(The Turks put a head on a stick by their door.)
No slickey boy'd venture in here for fear
He'd end up quite casually dumped on his rear.

Our locks and procedures are always first rate
With passes checked carefully at the front gate.
So where are my boots and my cigs by the carton?
And my buddy's whole stash, is it just forgotten?

How the hell can anyone do any more?
Well, the Turks put a head on a stick by their door...

CRASH

Do deer go to heaven?
You would think not.
That road's just for people
And an occasional tot.

Then what of the way
Something happened today,
When my wife hit a deer
As she drove through the park?

It was dark, and it leaped,
But it didn't quite clear...
So she sat in the driveway
In mortal fear.

Did the deer go to heaven,
Or was it still,
Was it still on the roof
Of her RX7?

RIDE

life is such a delicious ride
but not as sweet if you sit in back
you can laugh with the breeze
and the sun in your face
or huddle in back
with the windows closed
you can hope and hug
and smile and love
or frown back there
with the windows closed
life is such a delicious ride
here...stand by me
as the world slides by
come savor the ride
it's delicious
and brief

WONDEROUS DAYS

wonderous days at last are come
unlike before
when naive choices
confused our hearts
and rolled the future out of focus
a future dulled
and often blurred by anger
or by tears
yet through it all we always sensed
somehow
someway
these perfect perfect days would come

DANA REEVE

She's gone now, too,
And it breaks our hearts.
The sound of pride,
The color of love,
The taste of a smile?

Our senses reel...
She was all these things,
Savior to him, example to us,
Soft as a rock,
Hard as a breeze.

She's gone now, too,
And it breaks our hearts...
Such a short time,
But to care so much...
We'll be gentle with her memory.

LEAVE THE CHILD ALONE

Walk through time
watching your way
through leavings
of what passed before...
a virus, an unexploded bomb,
the mouthing of incendiary words,
a death,
a lack of smiles.
Or crawl inside
the heart of a child,
unspoiled, unaware,
and find an easier path.
But even then,
our prompting and
your gradual awakening
will always slide you back
to the hot causticity
of living...
so persevere,
unless or until we
defang the world
and somehow learn
to leave the child alone.

STORY

memories construct your soul
none but you can know the whole

a partial story can be found
whenever lovers hold
that part they can
but even then
what's missing is profound

we know another only
by the fleeting bits of age
whose chapters wait for writing
or for turning page by page

the more we read
the more we need
to understand what's true
a story's only finished
when your memories are through

SNOWFALL

beauty and stillness
lie clear and clean
on fields of quiet snow
breathe deeply
feel past and present in a pause
as soundlessly
sharp crisp snowflakes
fall sparkling and star-like
with the radiance of being
landing on arm or cheek
pure white touches of joy
cup them in your hands
watch them melt into your flesh
then move along
remembering

LOSS

it is to begin
    this ending that you seek
it is to begin

it is to end
    this beginning that you've lost
it is to end

the longing
    and the pain
may simply hurt again

but it will end
    only when
it begins again

IF

if we had known
that we were one

that we were one
since first we met

our paths would then
have been the same

our hearts together
all these years

but now we talk
and cannot touch

and talk again
but cannot see

and while I smile
to hear your laugh

I quietly ask...no...
sadly say

how could we both
have been so blind

to not have known
that we were one

that we were one
since first we met

we should have known
we should have known

CATCHING A CLOUD

When it ended,
and I left,
I'd failed to see
what always was,
kissing a moving shadow,
catching a rolling cloud.

Had I stayed,
can you imagine
what wonders might have been...
how we'd grasp the wind
and laugh and love
and hug the falling rain?

Now, if it's over, truly over,
for us both,
then tell me why
I still feel you
with each breath I take,
and see you in my mind.

This is the miracle I've sought:
for us to love and dance once more
within each other's memories
in a perfect, quiet place
where our hearts are always open
to amazing, wide-eyed dreams.

CONNECTION

woven from
filaments of infinite length
a strong fragile connection
hums like a tight string
carrying memories
of what our lives
once were

here near the end
the connection holds
as our dreams
decipher and interpret
the vibrations
struck by two hearts
so many years ago

and a truth is quietly revealed

the string still hums
with deep and elemental love

BACK THEN

It was a lifetime
in a few years...
everything
was new,
everything
about you...
the way you stood,
the way you smiled,
the sound of your voice,
your hand in mine,
and how silk
and warm
and soft
you felt...
all new.
Perhaps the newness
was the charm, but
it was all tacked to my brain then,
and now, no longer new,
it's been rummaged through
again and again
with bits and pieces
missing here and there
over time
and I just can't tell
anymore
which digs deeper,
the memory...
or its loss.

STAGES

When was the first time
I bundled up and trudged outside
into snow up to my elbows,
unable to move,
only able to laugh
until frozen tears
hung from my chin,
then later to run
back inside to stand over
the coal stove
trying to thaw out?

When was the first time
I rode a bike, feeling
the sweet control and
heady confidence of
finally doing something
on my own? Even
the ultimate crash
and bloody aftermath
couldn't tarnish the
effort or the result
or spoil the feeling.

When was the first time
I saw you, held you,
kissed you...
loved you?

We were so young,
and everything was
so fragile...
then I spoiled the feeling,
lost my balance and
it ended
with our frozen tears.

KISS

Your soft kiss
made me
crawl inside myself
and purr. Its
perfection
was a slow place
that time could not
touch...the rhythms
too relaxed and
careful for hours
even to measure.
When it ended
(if it did)
it could not end.
It was forever
imprinted
and lasting...
a small thing,
much too small
to change the world,
only big enough
to change my life.

LATE-AUGUST GRASS

stopped on the old dirt road
our sight taken by the hillside
covered with late August grass
tall as a woman's hips
swaying in a golden dance
millions of separate pieces
responding and moving together
in the light breeze

carefully finding our way
down the hill through the hay
to a soft spot in the middle
where we lay hand in hand
watching small white clouds
drift lazily and then
responding and moving together
in the light breeze

WEDDING PRAYER

let's dream together you and I
leaving old things where they lie
the years have flown and we've missed so much
a kiss...a hug...a gentle touch
but finally together at last we can
see the future as a plan
that runs to heaven for us both
side by side a second growth
of hope and trust and endless love
sparkling with joy like the stars above
we'll pray for nothing more than this
and seal our dream with a lingering kiss

WHERE DID LOVE GO

we lost it one time ago
one long long time ago
inexcusable I guess
but we were kids
and we misplaced it
there was no way to know
when I left
that I'd spend years looking
only to realize finally
it's right here
all this time
it's been right here
right behind your smile

SOMEDAY

I didn't know it would end
didn't know it could
if I had looked far ahead
and had seen us where we are now
choices might have changed
but a half century later
memories are still clear and sharp
and a beautiful young girl still lives in my mind
and bubbles to the top once or twice a day
and I remember her saying: someday
well someday never came
maybe the dream alone
gave more substance to our lives
than would the harsh presence of reality
perhaps our lives apart
with the generation of two families
was worth the price

but nat king cole can sing once more
the alewife stream can rush and roar
the black and white can hiss with snow
as I hold your hand in mine
and I at last can hear you say:
it's here it's here someday is here

LOVE-SONG

your love came lightly into my heart
into my soul
and should be inside me now
singing
but when I close my eyes
it's still
and the silence is of other days
other times
when I was held by another
and you were just a dream
but if I listen close
this stillness
though unexpectedly real
whispers unheard tunes
whispers wait
wait for me

SAVORING THE JUICE

when someday comes
we'll hold each other
and chew up life
tasting the beauty
swallowing the sweet
we'll chew up life
and savor the juice

BEHIND THE YELLOW LINE

in a rumble of sound and motion
the subway car stops
you enter
as I step off
and we touch lightly
quick smiles on unknown faces
but a hollow meeting
for now I stand behind the yellow line
and dare not cross to take your hand
the line is meant to keep us from
an accidental trip to nowhere
the line is meant to keep us safe
will you remember me
I'll remember you
or not

LEAVING

crying doesn't do it
another time
perhaps

but not now

looking back
blankly
where she stands

as the bus pulls out

crying just won't do it
not when
something ends abruptly

foreshortened

emptied

mean

not unless
or only if
but never now

oh well
perhaps
another time

BORLAND HALL

Once home of a sea captain,
Large for the neighborhood,
Perfect, now, for three kids growing up
To learn the world is not always sunny.
Standing a half mile from the river
That plowed quickly to the sea
Leaving beauty in its path
And oyster shells
Heaped and shining on its banks
With little bones blatantly interspersed,
Perhaps from a weighted bag
Of newborn kittens
Thrown from the bridge late at night,
It was a place where someone standing
On the back step could shoot birds,
Or whatever moved, just for fun,
Or lie in bed remembering
The classmate, late for school,
Who forgot his wallet, drove home,
Lost five minutes, then met
An eighteen-wheeler head on.
Borland Hall...from a window you might see
A trapper leaving bloody ovals
In the clean, fresh snow
As he snowshoed home.

Borland Hall...sanctuary of hope,
Refuge of dreams, place of
Asylum.

GLIDDEN STREET

The floor was not level...
A ball bearing dropped
While loading a new slingshot
Would roll faster and faster
Until it was stopped
By the opposite wall.
We'd laugh and do it again,
Then run to the attic
Where, hanging from the trapeze,
We'd have a view
Of Dad's new Studebaker
Or the postman with his bag
Bringing mail and the newspaper
He'd picked up out front.
He'd smile up at us
And chat about kid things...
Never about the war.

We got letters from him for a year
On paper with lines through important stuff,
But that stopped one day,
After Iwo Jima, I think.
An unimportant life
With a line through it...
But important enough
To make us angry enough
To spit in the river
Where we weren't supposed to be,

Resulting in our inability
To sit for a while.

But we weren't angry enough
To remember very long.

CHINA VILLAGE

named for a baptist hymn
not the country

home to my father
when he went to colby college
just eight or ten miles away
and site of his hazing
when city born fraternity brothers
blindfolded him one dark night
then drove into what they supposed
was an unknown part of the maine wilderness
where they droped him off

he removed the blindfold
looked around
then walked up the driveway
to his house
went upstairs and went to bed

he dreamt of the easy
laid-back life in china village
where only occasional bursts
of exceptional novelty

would strike interesting patterns
in an otherwise graticulated world

like the burning of his father's country store
just down the street

which went up like a fuel dump
since for years one of the items sold there
was kerosene
pumped in a back room
from tanks that constantly leaked
on the wooden plank floor and
down through cracks
into the dirt below

after the store finished burning
the earth itself burned for another week

my grandfather never rebuilt
he retired and died one time
on a trip to florida

then someone did build another store
at the other end of town
did well until his financial ineptitude
caused a midnight abandonment

later rodents were noticed outside
and inspectors found the place was overrun
since when he departed
the owner left all the food inside

one man when he looked in
saw a rat on a shelf calmly eating a snickers bar

I think this might have been a rat worth knowing

CHINA LAKE

something with wings (a wasp perhaps)
brushes my mind stirring memories long forgotten
when careless days went slow so slow
and the tall hay raked and taken to the barn
became a playground for us to leap into
(watch out for the pitchfork)
then running with the pungent hay
sticking to and into our sun-browned skin
down to the lake to swim easily for miles
(at least we thought so)
or to slide on an outhouse door
behind a speedboat driven by a deaf woman
who never heard us yell when we fell off
thus going the length of the lake before she knew
and then to lie on the dock in the sun laughing
and picking off an occasional bloodsucker
or chasing away that pesky wasp
with the smell of lobster and corn cooking by the shore
in fifty-five gallon drums cut lengthwise
and a waitress finding some city people
preferred steak (imagine that)

the sweetness of living is always there
even behind pain
it simply needs the whisper of wings
to be again

NORTHERN LIGHTS

It had rained again, a cold October rain,
But stopped now at sunset…
A frosty mist rising, undisturbed, from the warm lake,
And smoke from the cabin standing straight as a pole.
Walking along the shore, gathering dry wood for the fireplace,
He stepped over rivulets of rainwater
That made small channels to the lake
And carried invisible bits of life,
A kind of magical necessity,
Like the blue veins on the backs of his aging hands.

The night now sharply crisp and clear,
With stars and stars and more stars overhead,
All soon to be lost
As the Northern Lights made their slow, brilliant,
Crawl across the sky.
Walking, then, to the cabin,
Alone, battling sameness,
Waiting for his time, not fearing it anymore…
Just as he hadn't minded not being born,
So many years before.

THE LAKE

not a whisp of air moves
the clear surface of the lake
it's spread out like a blue sheet
pulled army tight
and yesterday's memories
seem to bounce off
like spinning dimes
beneath lie parts of other days
wedding rings and tires
rubbers and weeds
a universe of forgotten jetsam
should we launch our boat
and disturb this perfect cover
or stand quiet and still
and just watch from the shore?

RAIN

from time to time
the sound of rain
makes a picture in my mind
of a kid years ago
huddled on the stairs
so scared
even with pillows over his head
the thunder
seemed a live thing
intent on devouring only him
the cabin by the lake
way too flimsy to save him
and of course
the others didn't help
when they laughed at him

LANDING ANOTHER EEL

Feigning indifference
as he cast from the boat
he watched his line
initially float
then reluctantly sink
in the depths of the lake,
where, darkly invisible,
a kind of fierce snake
slid through the weeds
to collide with the bait...
a careless response
to a barbed, baited hook.

It climaxed as war
and radically shook
the line, rod and fisher
who hurriedly asked:
Can I breathe under water?
Can I walk on the wet?
Can I handle the squirming?
Is the hook firmly set?
Once the line and the catch
had been frantically fought,
he stood fearful to see
how much trouble he'd caught.

NIGHTFALL

evening light
ripples and slides
over the calm lake
softly outlining
the ghostly shape
of his small sailboat
anchored far from the float
where he stands now
hesitantly
measuring the way back

dare to dive
when it's nearly dark?

the water's warm
the boat is there
but darkness blinds
and the long crawl home
will cleave the surface
of an obscure
shifting world
that may grasp
and suffocate
a fearful soul

dare to swim
through the weeds at night?

IT□S A WONDER

in those days
we'd wash our hair
sitting on the end of the dock
using what was left
of an old bar of ivory soap
no problem if the soap
got in the lake

and we'd use noxema
after we burned
since there was nothing
to use before

and remember burning leaves
the sound
the smell
the sight?

it's a wonder we survived

BLACK FLIES

late May the ice out three weeks
the cold still holding the lake
in a blanket of gray wet drizzle
we had bundled up and fished the deep end
hoping for togue or bass or even perch
but hours later nothing

some warmth as the sun broke through
and then as we fished near shore
trying to free an errant line
an immense cloud of sound
as black flies coming down off a hill
found us before we found our fish

or freed the line

DRAGONFLY

Fly that once was killer nymph,
dragon without lair,
you who rests benignly now,
on gentle gusts of air,
can you recall that sudden point
'tween after and before
when you were neither good nor bad
but both and something more?
You had no choice but to become
a dragon without fire,
but given choice might you prefer
to reach for something higher,
to be, perhaps, mosquito-hawk
or a wing-ed blue snake-eater?
But no, I'm sure if you could talk
you'd probably pick neither,
instead you'd dive among your prey,
and in the deep cause much dismay
as you assumed your evil side,
and resumed your frantic minnocide.

A PERFECT STONE

Sure of what she had found
at the lake edge,
she stood for a moment,
ready to touch,
suddenly hesitant...
afraid she might cause
a jolt to the tilt
and the turn of the earth.
She recalled summers
as they skipped rocks
on the calm lake,
remembering his bold throw,
a singular form
of pure delight.
And they had always searched
for that one perfect stone,
a natural marvel that,
when thrown with a sidearm spin,
would skip perfectly,
unlike the forced skipping
of common rocks.
Now, looking at this stone,
she knew without touching
that an average throw
would launch it to eternity.
But, since he was no longer there
to throw, to watch, to smile,
and realizing that this stone

was only there to find
and not to use,
she covered it with weeds,
and left it there,
unmoved.

CASTING OFF

our canoe clears the dock
hardly disturbing the sheen
of the early morning calm
the sun so warm
and the lake so smooth and flat
you feel you can get out and walk
on its clear transparency

over there
she held a guest's head
above the surface
until help came
years ago
and out there
beyond the float deeper
another guest lost an outboard motor
when he forgot to tighten the clamps
and right here
I was hurt
when a starter rope
swollen by water
stuck in the flywheel
and the handle
hit me a hundred times
before I could move

in front of us now
the opening under the causeway

will let us through to a world
of lilly pads and dragon flies big as birds
and turtles and pond frogs and lush green life
but first we'll go by the place on the lake
where a friend dove off a rock in the shallows
broke his neck
and died

PAINTING THE LAKE

They gave me fifty cents
For my birthday when it came,
Then my grandfather and I
Would always play a game…
We'd put our heads together,
And conspire to paint the lake.

I'd often go for yellow,
Then old Gink would go for red,
And Grammie B, dear four eyes,
Might pick lavender instead.

Each year we'd laugh and fool around,
Until at last we'd find,
The only way to paint the lake
Was to do it in your mind.

So now I'm close to their age,
After years and years of change,
And anyone who knows me
Doesn't really find it strange,
That now and then I take a break,
And go off to paint the lake.

A CHOICE OF DREAMS

dream of storms
gales
blowing seas
and heaving

white waves
all the while
lying snug
in your warm bed

in a cabin
by a calm lake
or toss and turn
in a ship's cabin

running before
that violent sea
dreaming of that
peaceful lake

where you are
and what you are
may be simply
a choice of dreams

PORPOISE

its carefree leap
tears open

the interface

and creates
a momentary entrance

to the sky

then the quick fall back
and joyous splash

a reconciliation

since nothing heals faster
than the broken surface

of the sea

OCEAN STAGE

the play begins
as we watch from the shore
near sundown
a truly magnificent cloud
bursting over
the ocean stage
its white arms flung upward
into the red-gold sky
conducting
waves birds sounds
and a ship leaving
through wisps
of a perfect day
its lights disappearing
as it quietly sails
way beyond the reach of land
and we know
passengers will see
looking back
our own lights dim
as the stage fades to black

ARRIVAL

The geese arrived
at five forty five
with little truck horns
clearing the sky.

We stood sad and forlorn
as the many foul fowl
splashed down on the pond
and crawled out on the lawn.

We cringed at the sight
of the dumb poop machines
ignoring our plight
and destroying our dreams

as our offal free lives
were filled up once more
with a burden of muck
that caused shoes to be sucked

off our tentative feet.
So we hurriedly beat
a hasty retreat
to the warmth of our house.

We hid until sure
they weren't there anymore.

WONDERLAND

Suppose the world were real one day,
suppose, suppose for once,
our measure ran from noon to noon,
and stars appeared for lunch.

This kind of thing might happen, say,
if walking through the rain,
the hard, transparent underlay
beneath a water pool

should pop and tear
and whoosh you through
with arms and eyes askew.
And down you'd go,

or is it up?
No matter, you'd be there,
within a topsy-turvey world
that lies beneath our care.

And in that world
of strange old things,
you'd marvel at the view,
for old to you would seem quite new

until at last you learned
that people there
speak with their hearts,
and laugh with pain at love.

Suppose the world were real one day,
suppose, suppose for once,
that people saw with mind and soul,
and stars appeared for lunch.

CULL

light illustrates the sky
with a reddish hint
of coming night

the hunter waits carefully
in his blind
above the shadows

and below
families of deer
fitfully seek the bait

he shoots straight down
no ricochets
no harm to the neighbors

just stillness
fading light
and dark dark blood

SPRING MELT

The last little fingers
of late winter snow
lie absolutely still,
caught in their inability
to move further under the eves,
deeper into the shadows,
behind the trees.
Weeks ago
they boldly covered
fields and houses…
now, with no place to hide,
they're doomed by a warming sun.

WALK WITH ME

come walk with me on winding paths
that lead from there to here
and feel the joy of younger days
when all was new and clear
come walk with me and hold my hand
and know that while we cannot halt the flow of time
or stop its rush to harsh decay
together you and I can glide
through secret fields 'neath softening skies
where every day's a perfect day
that fills our soaring hearts
with endless dreams of warmth and light
and once again retards
the cold and darkness of approaching night

NOTHING LASTS

this song of life begins
composed of notes
from yesterday
a childhood laugh or cry
the shadow on the stair
a bump beneath the bed
a well-earned hug
a gentle touch of love
all bits and pieces
that create
the sharps and flats
of a symphony
a daring start
to life's full song
of soaring
trembling
ephemerality

UNEXPECTED THINGS

the end comes closer now
with its unexpected things
shards of glass
a leaking valve
accidental leanings
ice
should I guess which?
could I guess when?
it's best I think
simply to shrug and ramble on
for innocence
is an antidote to fear

REHEARSAL

if you look for me
I'll be lying down
just need to rest a bit
don't think I'll sleep
not yet
but I swear
life's getting harder
every day
comforter to my chin
hands on my chest
legs straight
I'll lie perfectly still
in the coolness
rehearsing

DREAMER

and now three score and ten
I marvel at how fast it's been
through school marriage kids the rest
time snapped its fingers almost in jest
and caused the world to hurtle by
no sense for me to question why
I finally realize how it works
because of nature's little quirks
I've been awake for forty-seven
and sound asleep for twenty-three
which means in essence don't you see
I'm one third dreamer
two thirds me

THE WICKED THING

it's not too late to dream
if there is just one minute left
that's time enough
that's time enough

the wicked thing
the awful thing
is not to dream at all

so join with me and clear the haze
look inward where dreams lie
see everything and anything
imagine what can be

the wicked thing
the awful thing
is not to dream at all

SHADOW

imitation of substance
you have none of your own
mimic of motion
you are bound to be moved
your existence depends
upon me not you
yet you die sometimes
while I live
and you'll live
perhaps
when I die

CONUNDRUM

when you are passed
here on earth
by others traveling
a similar path
pressing harder or relenting
is usually determined by
who's doing the passing
an impossible decision
when love's involved

FLOATING TO JERUSALEM

this is the way it could happen
this is the way it might be

a sapling uprooted by nature
from its lush fertile home near the sea
somehow someway finds the ocean
and slowly but surely floats
to the west to the sun to the start of it all
then years and many years later
it stands in the desert sand
waiting and watching history
waiting for time to be right
then uprooted by turmoil and freed once more
it finds its way back to the sea
and slowly but surely floats again
steadily back to its home

if you stand in the redwood forest
you can stand in awe and think
one of these trees had a vision
one of them knows far more
than all of the world's religions
for one of these trees was there

LOOKING FOR HEAVEN

they lie perfectly still
on their backs
in the grass
watching the underside of clouds
enjoying the careful movement
as shapes form
and dissolve
animals
things
abstract or not
never lasting long
like ghosts
but real for a minute
of course nothing is up there
it's all down here
isn't it?

A LASCIVIOUS THOUGHT

breaststroking in the androscoggin
is unwise
paper mills have suffocated the river
they've installed bubblers
so the fish won't die
but we can have a picnic
by the shore
and if you bring your breasts
I'll stroke them

SUNDAY MORNING

I lie in bed trying to find
a reason to get up
weekends are so long
and seem now to be
just lots of time to fill

at least before she died
there were things to do for her
and if you were here with me
you'd fill my world with love

but I lie here trying to find
a way to overcome
the absence of you both
and a reason to get up

AMERIQUE

I didn't set the alarm so the dog is dead
I didn't set the alarm so the dog is dead
I didn't set the alarm so the dog is dead
yesterday was king tut's birthday and
the boom echoed throughout the house
when I blew out the candles
so don't tell me how to push a button
now that the dog is gone
he would have yapped on the beach anyway
so why shouldn't I cry
I didn't set the alarm
so the dog is dead
damn it all to hell

SUNSET AT SEA

sun dazzled clouds
prismatic and capricious
line the vast horizon
where the sea and the sky meet
they shape limitless variations
that are timed with the iridescent rhythm
of the ocean's cerulean swells
then with a brief sizzling flare
the sun finally slips
over that distant watery cliff
and an ebony blanket
covers the sea

NEW CAR

this one's a beast
loaded with things
I never guessed I'd need
heated seats
along with separate zones
so I don't carelessly heat
someone's space
when they're not with me
and a button to push
that holds the car on a hill
so I don't need to exert myself
by pushing the brake
and a switch that automatically
turns on the headlights
so I don't need to remember
to do that when it's dark
and the best thing
you can talk to this beast
and it will find places and things for you
so I've been asking it to help
since I've got fog lights
and I can't find any fog

Nelson Ward Bailey, aka Sam Bailey, born August 3, 1936, Damariscotta, Maine, son of two teachers, brother of two sisters, friend of four cats and one dog...

Married Carol Sideris, July 1962, who died after a long illness February 2009. Daughter and one son live with their families in New Hampshire, another son and his family are in North Carolina. Five super grandsons and two delightful granddaughters.

Attended Boston University, graduated from Wesleyan University and Fairleigh Dickenson University. After practicing dentistry for 42 years, retired November 2012.

Wrote a few poems in the 1960's, nothing more until a few years ago. Never published.